Ficus Tr

Ficus Bonsai Tree

Written by Bernard Brook

The Complete Guide to Growing, Pruning and Caring for Ficus

Top Varieties: Benjamina, Ginseng, Retusa, Microcarpa, Religiosa, All Included

Published by

WHYTBANK PUBLISHING

ISBN: 978-0-9930278-0-2

Foreword

If you are looking for the perfect houseplant to add intrigue and liven up your home, consider the ficus! With over 800 species to choose from you are sure to find one that meets your needs. Ficus trees produce lush green leaves and flexible trunks that can be bent, shaped and braided into nearly any shape imaginable – they also make great bonsai trees!

In this book you will learn the basics about ficus trees including their origins and history as well as information about the most popular species. You will also receive a detailed guide for starting ficus from seed, nurturing the saplings and caring for adult ficus trees (including bonsai varieties) at home. If you are ready to start growing ficus trees at home, keep reading!

Acknowledgements

I would like to extend my sincerest thanks to my family who have always supported me in my writing endeavors.

Special thanks to my wife and children for their endless patience and understanding with me.

Table of Contents

Chapter One: Introduction

The name "ficus" is given to a genus of woody trees and shrubs containing about 850 different species. The trees belonging to this genus are collectively known as fig trees or figs – the fruit they produce are known by the same name. While ficus trees (or fig trees) are an important source of food for wildlife and the fruits are often eaten as bushfood, these trees are primarily used ornamentally and trained as bonsai trees.

What makes the ficus tree so popular is the fact that there are hundreds of species to choose from and many of them are very hardy. Ficus trees come in all shapes and sizes, providing years of lush foliage if cared for properly. For the most part, these trees are easy to care for indoors and they can even be propagated at home.

If you are looking for a hearty and attractive plant to liven up your home, consider the ficus. These beautiful trees produce vibrant green leaves and unique trunks that can be bent, trained and shaped into braids. For those who are interested in a bonsai tree, several species of ficus trees make great options.

In this book you will learn the basics about ficus trees including what they are, where they come from and what the most popular species are. You will also receive a detailed guide for cultivating and caring for ficus trees (including bonsai varieties) in the home. If you are ready to start growing ficus trees at home, keep reading!

Useful Terms to Know

Deciduous – a type of plant that loses its foliage during the fall/autumn each year

Epiphyte- a type of plant that grows on another plant but does not act as a parasite

Evergreen – a plant that stays green during all four seasons; does not lose its foliage in fall/autumn

Hemiepiphyte – a plant that spends part of its life cycle as an epiphyte; seeds may germinate and develop as an epiphyte then the plant later becomes rooted in soil

Inflorescence - a grouping or clustering of flowers that grows from a main branch or stem

Ostiole – a tiny opening or hole in the inflorescence of fig plants through which pollinating wasps may enter

Shrub – a short tree-like plant, distinguished from a tree by its multiple stems

Syconium – a uniquely adapted type of inflorescence where the flowers are arranged on the *inside* of the enclosed receptacle

Symbiosis – a close and typically long-term interaction between two or more species in which the two depend on each other for survival

Temperate Zone – the region that lies between the subtropics and the polar circles; average yearly temperature is not extreme, neither hot nor cold

Tropical Zone – all areas on Earth surrounding the equator; generally warm to hot and moist all year round

Chapter Two: Understanding Ficus Trees

Because there are so many different species of ficus, there is a great deal to learn about them. In this chapter you will learn the basics about what the ficus is as well as interesting facts about its habitat, fruit, and pollination methods. You will also receive an overview about some of the most popular ficus trees kept as ornamental plants including the Common Fig, the Sacred Fig, the Weeping Fig, the Ginseng Fig, and the Chinese Banyan.

1.) What are Ficus Trees?

The name "ficus" is given to a wide variety of trees and shrubs belonging to the family Moraceae. There are about 850 different species of plant that carry the name ficus, but the plant that is most commonly referred to as a ficus is the Common Fig (*Ficus carica*). Later in this chapter you will learn the specifics about some of the most common species of ficus but, for now, you should learn about the ficus genus as a whole.

Plants belonging to the ficus genus can be found in tropical regions around the globe, though some species extend into the temperate zone. Many ficus plants are trees, but there are also shrubs, vines and epiphytes which carry the ficus name. Most species of ficus are evergreen because they live in tropical areas where the temperature never gets cold enough for them to lose their leaves. Those ficus plants which grow in more temperate zones and at higher elevations, however, are more likely to be deciduous. Deciduous ficus plants are usually endemic to certain regions outside of the tropical zone.

a.) Pollination of Ficus (or Fig) Trees

While differentiating between different species of ficus can be difficult, it is fairly easy to identify this group of plants as a whole. Ficus plants, figs more specifically, have aerial roots – they also grow in very distinct shapes which make it easy to distinguish them from other plants. Another unique feature of fig trees is that they display inflorescence – a grouping or clustering of flowers that grows from a main branch or stem. The pollination system for fig trees is also very unique.

The fruit of fig trees is enclosed in an inflorescence and it is sometimes referred to as a syconium - a hollow, fleshy stem that contains multiple ovaries inside and several flowers outside. Pollination of fig trees is only accomplished by tiny fig wasps (wasps belonging to the family Chalcidoidea) which enter the enclosed inflorescences through a tiny ostiole. Inside the inflorescence, the wasps pollinate the fruit and lay their own eggs. In this way, fig wasps and ficus trees have a sort of symbiotic relationship – they both rely on the other for life.

b.) Uses for Ficus Trees

In many rainforest ecosystems, ficus trees are a keystone species – a species which has a significant effect on the ecosystem simply due to its abundance. The fruit of the ficus (or fig) tree is an important food source for a number of frugivore species including bats, capuchin monkeys, langurs and various birds including pigeons, hornbills and barbets. Various types of insects also rely on the fig tree for food, feeding on its leaves or wood. The Giant Swallowtail butterfly (*Papilio cresphontes*) and many caterpillars belonging to the order Lepidoptera rely on fig leaves for food while the larvae of the citrus long-horned beetle (*Anoplophora chinensis*) feed on its wood.

In addition to acting as a food source for many rainforest species, ficus trees also provide food for humans. Several species of ficus are cultivated for their fruit while others are used for their wood. Throughout history, ficus trees have played a key role in many cultures, their use dating as far back as 9,200 BCE. You will learn more about the history of ficus trees in the next section.

c.) Fruit and Reproduction

As you have already learned, the fruit of ficus trees are called figs and they grow in a specialized structure called a syconium. The syconium is a uniquely adapted type of inflorescence where the flowers are arranged on the *inside* of the enclosed receptacle. This being the case, you cannot actually see the flowers of the fig tree unless you cut open the syconium. This is why the pollination of fig trees is so unique and interesting – fig wasps are specifically evolved to crawl into the syconium to access the flowers for pollination of the fruit.

The shape of the syconium is often bulbous at the bottom and pointed near the top where it connects to the branch. Depending on the species of ficus, fig fruits can contain anywhere between several hundred to several thousand seeds. Unless the fruit is pollinated, however, the ficus cannot reproduce through these seeds. If you cut open a fig, you will see what looks like hundreds of fleshy threads, each connected to a single seed.

2.) History of Growing Ficus Trees

Throughout human history, ficus trees have played an important role in many cultures. In ancient Egypt, the soft wood of fig trees was used to make mummy caskets. It is thought that certain species of ficus including the Common Fig (*Ficus carica*) and the Sycamore Fig (*Ficus sycomorus*) were some of the first plants bred deliberately for agriculture by humans. Historic evidence suggests that this began in the Middle East as long as 11,000 years ago. Fossilized figs have also been found dating back to early Neolithic villages from 9,200 BCE.

In addition to serving practical purposes, the fig tree has also played a prominent role in religious traditions of various human cultures. The oldest living plant (with a known planting date) is a Sacred Fig (*Ficus religiosa*) known as the Sri Maha Bodhi – it was planted in 288 BCE in the temple at Anuradhapura in Sri Lanka by King Tissa. The Common Fig is also a sacred tree in the religion of Islam – there is a whole chapter (called a Sura) in the Quran titled At-Tin, or "The Fig". Fig trees also have religious significance in Hinduism, Buddhism and Jainism.

Buddha himself, the figure on which the religion of Buddhism is founded, is said to have achieved enlightenment while meditating under a Sacred Fig tree. This same species is identified as the "world tree," or Ashvattha of the Hindu religion. The Sacred Fig is even mentioned in the Bible – in Genesis 3:7, Adam and Eve cover their naked bodies with fig leaves after the Fall/Autumn. There is also an instance in which Jesus curses a fig tree for bearing no fruit in Mark 11:12 – 14.

3.) Types of Ficus

There are over 800 species belonging to the ficus genus, but not all of them are commonly kept as house plants. Aside from the Common Fig (*Ficus carica*), <u>some other popular species include the following</u>:

Weeping Fig (*Ficus benjamina*)

Ginseng Ficus (*Ficus retusa*)

Chinese Banyan (*Ficus microcarpa*)

Sacred Fig (*Ficus religiosa*)

Common Fig (*Ficus carica*)

The Common Fig is a species of flowering tree native to areas of the Middle East and western Asia. This tree is widely cultivated for its fruit but it is also very popular as an ornamental plant. In the wild, this tree grows in dry, sunny areas with deep soil – it can also grow in rocky soil and at elevations up to 1,700 meters (5,577 feet). Though this species can grow in nutritionally poor soil, it requires well-drained soil to thrive.

This tree produces fragrant, deeply lobed leaves that grow 5 to 10 inches (12 to 25 cm) long and 4 to 7 inches (10 to 18 cm) wide. The tree itself grows to an average height of 23 to 33 feet (7 to 10 m) and has smooth, white bark. This species produces an edible fig which measures 1 to 2 inches (3 to 5 cm) long and has green skin that often ripens to a dark purple or brown color. The fruit of the fig tree can be used for a variety of culinary applications. It can be eaten fresh or dried, and it is often used to make jam. Ripe figs typically do not transport well, so most commercial production of the fruit is dried or processed in other ways. One of the most popular uses of this fruit is as a filling for the Fig Newton cookie produced by Nabisco, a version of the fig roll.

Weeping Fig (*Ficus benjamina*)

This species of ficus is known as the Weeping Fig or Benjamin's Fig, but it is commonly sold as a houseplant simply bearing the name "ficus". The Weeping Fig is a flowering tree native to Australia and Southeast Asia where, in natural conditions, it can reach a height of 98 feet (30 m). These trees have drooping branches full of glossy leaves that grow up to 5 inches (13 cm) long. This tree also produces small fruits that are highly favored by birds in its native habitat.

Though the fruit of the Weeping Fig is edible, that is not the main reason why it is cultivated. This species of ficus is popular for decorating urban parks and as a houseplant – it is also the official tree of Bangkok. What makes this tree so popular as a houseplant is its tolerance of poor growing conditions. Though this species prefers bright sunlight, it will survive in the shade and it only needs enough water to keep it from drying out. One thing to keep in mind with this species of ficus is that it can grow fairly large indoors, so pruning is recommended. You may also need to eventually swap its pot for a larger one as it grows.

Ginseng Ficus (*Ficus retusa*)

Also known as the Cuban Laurel, the Ginseng Ficus is an evergreen species of ficus native to the Malay Archipelago. This species grows very rapidly, forming a round, broad head of leaves. In proper conditions, this tree can grow up to 49 feet (15 m) tall with a spread just as wide. These trees have smooth grey bark and the trunk can grow to a diameter up to 3.3 feet (1 m). The size of the trunk is necessary to support the fast-spreading canopy of the tree.

The Ginseng Ficus produces glossy, dark green leaves that are oval in shape and alternate up the stem. New leaves, which are produced year-round, have a light rose color which, when contrasted to the dark green of mature leaves, gives the tree an attractive two-tone effect. The bark is typically grey in color, though it may have a reddish hue, and it is dotted with horizontal flecks called lenticles to promote gas exchange in the bark. Though popular as a houseplant in its traditional form, the Ginseng Ficus is more popular as a bonsai.

Chinese Banyan (*Ficus microcarpa*)

This species of ficus is known by several names including the Chinese Banyan, Indian Laurel, and the Curtain Fig. These trees are native to Asia, found throughout Sri Lanka and India as well as parts of the Malay Archipelago and the Ryukyu Islands. The Chinese Banyan can also be found in Australia. This species of ficus was first described in 1782 and, since then, several varieties of the species have been identified, all carrying the name *Ficus microcarpa*.

The Chinese Banyan achieves an average height around 40 feet (12 m) with a spread of the same width, or greater. These trees prefer full sun and they can be hardy in temperatures as low as 25°F (-4°C). Chinese Banyan trees produce lustrous, oval-shaped leaves and small fruits in the form of a yellow-green nut. The bark of this tree is smooth and grey with lenticels on the smaller branches. An interesting fact about this species is that it is very easy to propagate through vegetative cutting.

Sacred Fig (*Ficus religiosa*)

The Sacred Fig tree is native to various parts of Asia including Nepal, India, Myanmar, Pakistan, and Sri Lanka as well as parts of China and Indochina. In India and Nepal, the tree is known as the Peepal or Pippal – it is also known as the Bo-Tree. The Sacred Fig is a large deciduous or semi-evergreen species that grows up to 98 feet (30 m) tall with a trunk diameter up to 10 feet (3 m). This tree produces cordate leaves that grow up to 7 inches (18 cm) long and 4.7 inches (12 cm) wide with an extended drip tip. The fruits are small figs measuring 0.6 inches (1.5 cm) in diameter.

The most interesting thing about the Sacred Fig is that it is considered to be sacred by the followers of various religions including Buddhism, Hinduism, and Jainism. Various parts of the tree have also been used in traditional medicine for a wide variety of conditions including diabetes, asthma, epilepsy, infections, and inflammatory disorders. The leaves of this tree also serve as a laxative and as a treatment for jaundice.

The Sacred Fig is primarily cultivated as an ornamental tree for use in gardens and parks, though it can also be used as an indoor houseplant. These trees prefer hot, humid weather and full sunlight. Though this tree prefers loam, it is capable of growing in most soil types. Proper watering and a pH below 7.0 is recommended to help this plan thrive indoors.

Chapter Three: What to Know Before You Grow

Now that you know some of the basics about ficus trees, including some of the most popular varieties, you may be ready to move into the specifics. Before you go out and buy a ficus tree, however, there are a few more things you should consider. Will you be keeping your ficus inside or outside? Should you keep a traditional ficus tree or go for a bonsai? And what are the pros and cons of ficus trees over other houseplants? You will learn the answers to these questions and more in this chapter.

1.) Indoors vs. Outdoors

When thinking about whether to plant your ficus tree outdoors or to keep it potted indoors, there are a number of factors to consider. <u>These factors may include</u>:

- <u>Temperature requirements</u>
- <u>Soil needs</u>
- <u>Lighting requirements</u>
- <u>Water and humidity</u>
- <u>Growth rate</u>
- <u>Susceptibility to pests</u>

Temperature Requirements

The key factor to consider in thinking about planting a ficus outdoors is the temperature – how cold does it get where you live? While the specifics vary from one species of ficus to another, most species are hardy to a temperature around 30°F (-1°C), or just below freezing. In the U.S., this means that you can plant ficus trees outdoors in USDA hardiness zones 10 through 12. If the temperature gets lower than 30°F (-1°C), as it does in most parts of the U.K., do not plant your ficus outdoors.

DO NOT PLAN TO
(Maybe Porch)

Another thing to consider, however, is the possibility of keeping your ficus in a pot so you can leave it outside during the summer and bring it inside during the winter. This is a great option if you live outside the hardiness zone for ficus trees, but still want to use them ornamentally outside. If you do choose to keep your ficus outside for part of the year, be sure to bring it inside early enough – well before the first frost, which can sometimes take you by surprise!

OK

Soil Needs

This is one requirement that is uniform for most species of ficus tree – they require well-draining soil. This means that if your property is at the bottom of a hill or in a flood plain, it may not be the best choice for growing ficus trees outdoors. The make-up of the soil itself is not particularly important, as long as it provides adequate nutrition for your ficus. If the soil is not well-drained, then your ficus is likely to succumb to rot and will not thrive.

(NEED PROPER RECIPE)

Lighting Requirements

When kept indoors, ficus trees typically require bright but indirect sun – they may also thrive in partial shade as long as they get some sunlight during the day. When planted outdoors, however, ficus trees generally do well in direct sunlight – at least 6 hours per day for optimal growth. If you plan to keep your ficus outdoors during the summer and move it indoors during the winter, keep in mind that you may need to acclimatize the tree slowly back to full sunlight before you move it back outdoors after winter.

ONLY IN MY GARDEN Area

Water and Humidity

Most species of ficus tree are native to tropical or sub-tropical areas where the soil and the air stays moist. This being the case, you need to think about whether the conditions where you live will meet the needs of your ficus. Fortunately, most ficus trees are hardy enough to survive in less than ideal conditions, but they may not thrive. If you do choose to plant your ficus outdoors you may need to water it once a week until it settles in – after that, its root system will be established enough to store water during dry periods. You should keep an eye on the ficus, however, and water it if the leaves start to turn yellow or if they start to fall from the tree.

Growth Rate

When given adequate space to spread, most ficus trees grow very quickly – this is true even if you keep them indoors. Only grow a ficus tree outside if you have plenty of space for it to grow – both vertically and horizontally. Plant your ficus tree away from power lines and away from your house because many species can grow up to 50 feet (15.2 m) or taller. Some species have a spread of 30 feet (9 m) or more, as well. Good GRIEF !!

If you choose to grow your ficus tree indoors, you still have to consider its growth rate. While an indoor ficus will not likely achieve a height of 50 feet (15.2 m), it can still grow fairly large. Make sure you are able to provide your ficus with enough vertical space to grow and plan to repot it every few years to prevent it from becoming root-bound. For some species, you may need to repot every year.

Susceptibility to Pests

Another factor to consider in planting your ficus outdoors versus indoors is the prevalence of pests in your area. If you plant your ficus outdoors, there is a much larger possibility that it will be exposed to various diseases and insect pests.

These things can still happen indoors, but they are less likely as long as you provide the proper growing conditions for your ficus. Certain pests are more prevalent in certain regions – for example, red mites tend to prefer hot, dry areas. Do a little research about the common pests in your area and compare it to the information provided in Chapter Six to see whether it is worth the risk of planting your ficus outdoors.

a.) Steps for Planting a Ficus Outdoors *NOT a good idea*

Though it is generally recommended that you keep ficus plants potted as indoor plants, you have the option of planting your ficus tree outside. If you choose to do so, follow these steps to plant your ficus correctly:

1. Purchase a ficus tree that looks hardy and healthy – if you start with a plant that is not in optimal condition, it is unlikely to do well outside.

2. Keep the ficus outdoors in a shady area for 2 to 3 days before planting it and keep the soil moist.

3. During this time, expose the tree to full sunlight for a few hours at a time, increasing the exposure each day – this will help acclimatize the tree to full sunlight without shocking it.

4. Choose an area for your ficus in full sun or partial shade that has well-drained soil.

5. Dig a large hole about three times the diameter and the same depth of the planter currently housing your ficus tree.

6. Carefully remove the ficus from the planter and place it upright in the center of the hole.

7. Gently loosen the roots to make it easier for them to spread – if the tree is root bound, cut about ¼ of the way into the bottom of the root ball to free the roots.

8. Fill in the hole around the ficus tree with native soil, packing it gently to remove pockets of air – do not fill the hole higher than the crown of the root ball.

9. Drive a tall stake into the ground beside the trunk and tie the trunk to the stake – the stake should be driven

at least 18 inches deep.

10. Spread several inches of mulch around the base of the ficus to help keep the soil moist – replace the mulch annually.

11. Water the area deeply until the soil and the roots are moist then keep watering at least once a week as the soil dries.

12. Fertilize the tree once a month between spring and fall/autumn with diluted all-purpose fertilizer – wait two weeks after planting the ficus to start fertilizing.

2.) Traditional vs. Bonsai Ficus

Not only do you need to think about whether you want to grow your ficus indoors or outside, but you also have to decide between growing a traditional ficus or a bonsai. Though a bonsai is essentially a ficus kept in miniature, the care requirements are very different. On the following page you will receive some basic information to consider in deciding between a traditional and a bonsai ficus.

Considerations for Traditional Ficus

- Require large pots and a dedicated position in a sunny area
- May be susceptible to drafts and cold weather (even when kept indoors)
- Generally very hardy in terms of soil quality and temperature as long as it is above freezing
- Most species do not require much pruning
- Re-potting is generally required every 1 to 3 years to give the plant room to grow
- Fertilization is recommended during the growing season (spring and summer months)
- Can be started from seed or propagated from cuttings

Considerations for Bonsai Ficus

- Can be kept in small pots, do not require a great deal of space
- Pruning and "bud nipping" required to maintain the size and shape of the bonsai
- Variety of different growing styles to choose from, opportunities for creativity
- You can train the tree and control its shape as desired
- May be more sensitive to changes in temperature

- Requires careful watering to avoid over- or under-watering (over-watering causes root rot)
- Fertilization may help spur growth but may also dry out the soil faster
- Can be started from seed and moved into its own pot when it is large enough

If the information above isn't enough to help you make an informed decision between a traditional and a bonsai ficus, keep reading. Throughout this book you will find more in-depth information about both options to help you decide which is the right choice for you.

3.) Pros and Cons of Ficus Trees

After reading a little bit more about ficus trees, you may be wondering whether or not it is really the right plant for you. With so many houseplants to choose from, you should not feel like your options are limited. Even within the ficus genus alone you have hundreds of different choices. In this section you will receive information regarding the pros and cons of keeping ficus trees ornamentally:

Pros for Keeping Ficus Trees:

- Variety of different species to choose from – each has a unique appearance
- Can be trained into different shapes according to your personal preference
- Generally very hardy when kept indoors, as long as its basic needs are met
- Can withstand a range of temperatures as long as it stays above freezing
- Accepts a range of soil quality as long as it is well-drained (should be kept in a deep pot with holes in the bottom)
- Generally does not require much pruning or trimming

Cons for Keeping Ficus Trees:

- Tend to grow fairly large, may require a good deal of space in the home (especially vertical space)
- May grow quickly, necessitating annual repotting (generally every 1 to 3 years)
- Needs fairly high humidity to thrive – you may need to mist the plant daily
- Can be finicky about watering needs – too little may cause dehydration while too much will cause rot
- Regular (monthly) fertilization is recommended during the growing season (spring and summer)
- Should not be kept in direct sunlight (or outdoors) unless it has been properly acclimated

SpRAY BoTTLE NEEDED

Chapter Four: Growing Ficus Trees Indoors

Though ficus trees can be found growing outdoors in their natural habitat, when kept ornamentally they tend to do best indoors. Like all houseplants, ficus trees have specific requirements in regard to lighting, temperature, and watering. In this chapter you will learn about the basic requirements for ficus trees as well as some species-specific information. You will also learn about fertilizing, propagating, and pruning ficus trees.

1.) Ideal Conditions for Growth

Because there are several popular species of ficus tree and each comes from a different geographical location, the information in this section is meant to provide general instructions for ficus care. At the end of this section you will find species-specific information regarding the ideal growing conditions for the five most popular ficus varieties: the Common Fig, Weeping Fig, Ginseng Ficus, Chinese Banyan, and the Sacred Fig.

a.) Light and Positioning

Most ficus trees require bright light in order to thrive. This being the case, it is recommended that you place your ficus plant near a large window that receives sunlight for several hours a day, though not all day. Unless they are acclimatized to direct sunlight, ficus trees can suffer from too much direct sunlight. You may also choose to place your ficus tree outdoors on a covered porch or patio during the summer months, as long as it doesn't get too hot or too cold.

Placing your ficus tree near a window is not the only consideration you need to make. You also need to think about other indoor conditions which might affect your plant. Your ficus should not be placed near heating or cooling vents, for example, because widely varying temperatures could negatively affect the plant. As long as the plant is positioned a few feet away from heating or cooling vents and away from drafts, however, it should be perfectly fine.

b.) Temperature and Humidity

Though different species of ficus have different preferences in regard to temperature, the average range is between 65° and 75°F (18° to 24°C). Your ficus may be okay with temperatures as low as 60°F (15°C) for short periods of time, but prolonged exposure to low temperatures will not be good for the plant. If you live in an area that gets very cold in the winter, you should keep your ficus in a room that is heated. You may also want to move your ficus further from windows and doors during the winter (as long as it still gets enough light) to prevent extreme temperature fluctuations.

Because many ficus varieties come from tropical or sub-tropical climates, they require a certain degree of humidity in order to thrive. In most cases, a ficus tree will survive in average humidity but there are several things you can do to increase the humidity for your ficus. One option is to mist the tree with water once or twice a day – you can also place a dish of warm water near the ficus tree. Humidity is particularly important for young ficus trees or if you have just moved it to a new location and it is going through an adjustment period. A third option is to install a humidifier in the room where you keep your ficus.

c.) Soil and Fertilizer

Ficus trees generally require some type of well-draining soil – planting the ficus in a deep pot with holes in the bottom will ensure proper drainage. These trees prefer loamy soil, which you can make yourself by mixing 3 parts of loam with 1 part of peat and 1 part of sand. This mixture will satisfy the ficus' needs for well-draining soil. It is important that you do not let the soil get too wet – see the next section for Watering Requirements.

In regard to fertilizing your ficus tree, you should only add fertilizer to the soil during the growing season (spring and summer). This is when the ficus will be putting out new leaves and branches, so the fertilizer will help to fuel this growth. During the growing season, use a general-purpose fertilizer diluted by 50% every three to four weeks. Ficus trees can be sensitive to fertilizers so, by using the fertilizer at half strength, you reduce the chances of it burning the plant. Do not fertilize your ficus during the winter.

It is also important to note that you will need to transfer your ficus to a new plot every one or two years, depending on the variety. Many ficus trees exhibit vigorous root growth and if they outgrow the pot, they may become root bound and will fail to flourish. When selecting a new pot for your ficus tree, choose one that is about 2 inches wider in diameter than the old pot so your ficus has room to spread. If you are purchasing a new ficus tree, you may want to replace the pot as soon as you bring it home.

d.) Watering Requirements

Most ficus trees can be found in naturally wet and humid conditions, so you should plan to keep the soil in your ficus' pot moist. It is important, however, that you do not let the soil get too wet and you must use a soil mix and a pot that allows the soil to properly drain. Only water your ficus when the top inch or two of soil have dried. During the summer, this will equate to about once-weekly watering. Make sure to place a tray beneath the pot to catch any excess water and discard the excess after watering the plant. After a few times you should get an idea how much water the plant will take.

e.) Species-Specific Requirements

Though the information provided in the previous pages will be adequate to care for a ficus tree indoors, you may want to make a few adjustments to your routine depending which species of ficus you choose. Below you will find tips for caring for the top five species of ficus tree:

Common Fig (*Ficus carica*)

This particular species of ficus is known for producing fruits and, if you care for it properly indoors, you can expect this to happen. The key to ensuring that your ficus produces fruit is to fertilize it properly during the growth season (spring and summer) and to make sure that the soil drains well and doesn't get too wet. When your ficus does produce fruit, wait until they are fully ripe to pick them.

Temperature: 65° to 75°F (16° to 24°C)

Lighting: well-lit area, but not direct sunlight

Humidity: daily misting is advised during the summer

Watering: allow the top 2 inches of soil to dry between watering

Soil: loamy, well-drained soil is best

Fertilization: once monthly between April and September, diluted to 50%

Repotting: as needed, every 1 to 2 years

Weeping Fig (*Ficus benjamina*)

This particular species of ficus is very hardy and not picky in regards to growing conditions. However, there are certain conditions in which it is most likely to thrive. This species of ficus prefers temperatures above 50°F (10°F) and enjoys a humidity level between 50 and 75%. If you notice the leaves of this plant starting to turn yellow, or if they are not growing to their proper size, you may need to add more fertilizer to the soil. If yellow spots appear on the leaves, it is a sign of overwatering so cut back for a while to let the soil dry out.

Temperature: 65° to 75°F (16° - 24°C), minimum 50°F (10°C)

Lighting: bright light but not all day, partial shade is best

Humidity: daily misting is advised during the summer

Watering: allow the top 2 inches of soil to dry between watering

Soil: fast-draining

Fertilization: once monthly between April and September, diluted to 50%

Repotting: only when necessary, every few years

Ginseng Ficus (*Ficus retusa*)

This species of ficus is evergreen which means it grows year-round in its natural habitat. When kept indoors, however, it is likely to go through a quicker growth period during the summer months and slow down in winter. The ginseng ficus does require higher humidity than some species, so plan to mist this plant once or twice daily and make sure that the soil drains well. This species tends to grow very quickly during the first few years in a new pot, but then it will slow down – once the growth slows, you will know it is time to replant the ficus in a bigger pot.

Temperature: 65° to 75°F (16° to 24°C)

Lighting: well-lit, but not in direct sunlight

Humidity: daily misting is advised during the summer

Watering: allow the top 2 inches of soil to dry between watering

Soil: fast-draining, recommended mix 30-40% organic matter and 60-70% aggregate

Fertilization: once monthly between April and September, diluted to 50%

Repotting: every few years

Chinese Banyan (*Ficus microcarpa*)

The root system of these trees swells to store water which means that you do not need to water these plants as much as some other species. When given adequate room to grow, this species will grow very quickly, so be ready to replace the pot every year or two. Chinese banyans tend to do best in medium light as long as they get some sunlight each day. Average temperatures are recommended with a minimum of 55°F (13°C).

Temperature: 65° to 75°F (16° to 24°C), minimum 55°F (13°C)

Lighting: medium light, some sunlight each day

Humidity: daily misting is advised during the summer

Watering: only when the top half of the soil dries out

Soil: soil-based potting mixture, fast-draining

Fertilization: once monthly between April and September, diluted to 50%

Repotting: every 1 to 2 years

Sacred Fig (*Ficus religiosa*)

This species of ficus tends to do well indoors as long as the temperature remains warm throughout the year. The sacred fig grows best when placed in bright indirect light, though it may also do well in partial shade with protection from hot afternoon sun. This species prefers soil-based potting mixes that drain well. It is especially important to avoid overwatering.

Temperature: 65° to 75°F (16° to 24°C)

Lighting: bright indirect light, partial shade

Humidity: daily misting is advised during the summer

Watering: allow the top 2 inches of soil to dry between watering

Soil: soil-based potting mixes that drain well

Fertilization: once monthly between April and September, diluted to 50%

Repotting: only when necessary, every few years

2.) Starting from Seed

Whether you plan to grow a traditional or a bonsai ficus, they all start from the same seeds. Starting a ficus from seed can be tricky and the process from seedling to mature tree will be a slow one, but it is well worth the wait. If you plan to train your ficus tree into a certain shape, raising it from seed may be a good option. Further, starting a ficus from seed enables you to have complete control over the growth conditions for its entire life so you can be sure to raise a healthy and hardy tree. On the following page you will find step-by-step instructions to raise ficus from seed:

1. Place the ficus seeds in a glass of water to separate the fertile from the sterile seeds

2. Any seeds that sink to the bottom are fertile – discard the sterile seeds that float on the top of the water

3. Fill a shallow plastic container with seed sowing mix (ideally a peat blend)

4. Press the fertile seeds gently into the surface of the sowing mix, but do not cover them

5. Water the seeds to moisten the soil then place the container outdoors in full sunlight or partial shade (the outdoor temperature must be at least 77°F (25°C)

6. If the outdoor temperature is too low, place the container indoors under artificial light

7. Keep the soil moist for the next 15 to 90 days – do not let it dry out

8. Once the seeds sprout a second set of leaves, transplant them into individual containers

*Note: Keep in mind that while the initial growth phase of ficus seeds and seedlings is slow, the plant will grow more rapidly after being transplanted to a new container. After transplanting your ficus seedling, continue to water it so the soils stays moist and make sure it has plenty of sunlight in warm weather.

3.) Feeding and Fertilizing

The ficus tree is naturally fast-growing. Because it grows so quickly, however, it needs additional nutrients to maintain this level of growth. Ideally, you should be feeding and fertilizing your ficus once a month during the growing season, or at least 2 to 3 times throughout the season. The growing season for ficus trees typically spans the warmer spring and summer months, though it may vary slightly depending where you live. In this section you will learn how to choose a fertilizer that will provide for your ficus' growing needs and receive tips for administering it.

a.) Choosing a Fertilizer

Before you can choose the right fertilizer for your ficus, you need to know what kind of nutrients it needs. The nutrients that plants require can be broken into three categories: macronutrients, micronutrients, and secondary nutrients. Macronutrients are the most important nutrients for general plant health – they include nitrogen, phosphorus, and potassium. Micronutrients are those which are required in smaller doses but are still necessary for good health – they include chlorine, boron, cobalt, copper, iron, manganese, molybdenum, nickel and zinc. Secondary nutrients are required in larger doses than micronutrients, but less than macronutrients – they include calcium and magnesium.

There are two different types of fertilizer: liquid and granular. The type you choose is largely a matter of preference. Liquid fertilizer is quickly absorbed and generally needs to be mixed with water for application. Granular fertilizers are applied to the soil dry and then watered to activate. This type of fertilizer is available in both quick-release and slow-release formulas. Most horticulturists agree that liquid slow-release fertilizer is typically best for ficus trees.

If you are looking for a good, all-purpose fertilizer that will work for your ficus trees, go with a complete 10-10-10 fertilizer. The numbers in this formula correspond to the amount of nitrogen, phosphorus, and potassium in the product. Given that all three numbers are the same, you know that a 10-10-10 fertilizer contains equal amounts of all three nutrients. This type of fertilizer will provide for your ficus' basic nutrient needs, but it may not be the best option available to you.

Ficus trees have particularly high needs for nitrogen, so you may want to choose a fertilizer that offers a higher ratio of nitrogen compared to the other nutrients. The ideal ratio for ficus trees appears to be 3:1:2 – that is, three parts nitrogen and two parts potassium for every 1 part phosphorus. Offering your ficus a fertilizer rich in nitrogen will help to stimulate the growth of healthy foliage.

b.) How to Fertilize a Ficus

The dosage and delivery method will depend what type of fertilizer you choose for your ficus. As a general rule, however, you should plan to fertilize your ficus once a month during the growing season – there is no need to fertilize during the winter when the ficus is dormant. When fertilizing ficus trees, it is generally recommended that you cut the recommended dosage in half to keep from burning the plant – this will also help to avoid the buildup of excess mineral salts in the soil.

When using a liquid fertilizer, you may be able to simply add the appropriate amount to your watering can when you water your ficus. For granular fertilizer, however, you will need to spread it on the soil around the root zone. Spread the fertilizer a few inches away from the trunk and sprinkle it evenly – do not dig it into the soil because you may disturb your ficus' shallow roots. After spreading the granular fertilizer, water the ficus well, drenching the soil to a depth of at least half the pot. If this ends up being more water than you usually offer your ficus, discard the water that drains into the container below the pot.

4.) Pruning and Training   Note pg 56

Because ficus trees tend to grow very quickly, you may need to prune it regularly. Pruning not only helps to control the vertical growth of the tree but, if you do it right, it can also help to encourage the tree to produce a fuller, lusher canopy. Keep in mind that pruning a traditional ficus is very different from pruning a bonsai – the information in this chapter applies to traditional potted ficus trees.

Below you will find a list of reasons for pruning a ficus:

- To inhibit or control excessive growth
- To enhance the appearance of the tree
- To condition the tree to take a certain shape
- To control or eliminate disease
- To remove dead leaves or branches
- To redirect nutrition to other parts of the plant
- To encourage new growth in spring (when pruned during dormancy)

Pruning a ficus tree is not difficult – all it may require is snipping a few leaves or twigs. For ficus trees, pruning is best done in the late summer or early fall/autumn after new growth has stopped. If you keep your ficus outdoors during the summer, prune it just before you bring it inside. If necessary, you can prune your ficus year-round but you are unlikely to have to prune more than a few dead or broken branches during the winter.

To prune your ficus tree you will not need any specialized equipment – just a pair of small pruning shears will do. There is no exact formula to follow in pruning your ficus – your aim should simply be to create a well-manicured tree that still looks natural. You might, for instance, remove the ends of branches that are growing higher than the main portion of the canopy. You might also remove twiggy stems growing out from the main trunk that make the ficus look messy. It is also best to remove any branches which are rubbing against each other and any branches which have died back. Err on the side of caution the first few times you prune your ficus so you don't remove too much. Eventually you will get the hang of it.

Follow these steps to prune your ficus: ♂ REMEBER

1. Locate the node where the twig or leaf you plan to remove meets the main branch or stem

2. Use the pruning shears to make a clean cut on a slight downward slant just above the node.

3. Cut as close to the node as you can without cutting into it, this is where the new growth will begin.

4. When planning your cuts, make sure to leave at least one node on the branch to allow for new growth

5. If you are removing an entire branch, cut it just before the limb or trunk – do not leave any nodes on the branch

*Note: Keep in mind that pruning too much of your ficus at once may result in a stress reaction. If your ficus suddenly drops all of its leaves after a major pruning, it could be a stress reaction. You do not need to be alarmed, however, because the leaves will eventually grow back and your ficus will adjust.

5.) Braiding a Ficus Trunk

Braiding a ficus trunk is a popular method of training a ficus tree and is much easier than it looks. It can be used for a traditional ficus or a bonsai ficus. Before you can start braiding, you need to have the suitable plant material. What you will need is 3 ficus seedlings of a similar size that have flexible trunks no wider than 1 inch in diameter.

Follow these steps to begin your braiding:

1. Plant your 3 seedlings close together in the middle of your chosen pot.

2. Insert 2 bamboo canes or stakes into your pot at either side.

3. Remove any small twigs or growth from the trunks of your seedlings. You want the trunks to be as smooth as possible.

4. Start your braid of the three trunks beginning at the bottom, they do not need to be very tight as they will grow and graft together.

5. Stop the braid just below the start of the foliage and tie loosely with a piece of garden twine, secure this on one of the stakes

6. As your tree grows, repeat the above steps until the braid is your desired height.

6.) Propagation Methods

Propagation methods for plants vary depending on the species and, for ficus trees, there are several options available. One option, seed propagation, has already been discussed in this chapter. In this section you will learn the basics about three other methods of ficus propagation: tissue culture, stem cuttings, and air layering.

a.) Tissue Culture

This method of ficus propagation is typically used for commercial ficus production – it is not something you are likely to do at home. Tissue culture involves collecting a sample of plant tissue and then growing it under sterile conditions in a growth medium. This procedure essentially results in the cloning of the plant and it is also referred to as microropagation. Some of the benefits of tissue culture propagation over other methods include:

- Producing clones of plants that have particularly desirable traits
- Quickly produces mature plants without seeds
- Does not require pollination
- Reduced risk for transmission of disease or pests

b.) Air Layering

Also referred to as marcotting, air layering is another method through which plants like the ficus can be propagated. The layering process involves planting an aerial stem (while still attached to the plant) so it can put out roots and then be detached as an independent plant. In their native habitat, layering is a means by which ficus trees may propagate naturally. Air layering is a slightly different process than traditional layering.

In air layering, a stem is wounded – a strip of bark may be removed to expose the inner tissues of the plant. The wound is then encased in a rooting medium (often sphagnum moss) and surrounded by a moisture barrier, such as plastic. Eventually, roots will grow from the wound and the stem can then be severed from the parent plant and planted in the ground. It may take several weeks for the wound to produce roots or, in some cases, an entire growing season.

c.) Stem Cuttings

The most common method for propagating ficus trees at home is using stem cuttings. This process simply involves removing a portion of the parent plant, letting it sprout new roots, and then planting it in a new pot. Like layering, this propagation results in a clone of the original plant. This method is the easiest to employ at home.

Unfortunately, stem cutting propagation can be a little tricky because cuttings are at risk for dehydration. Cuttings have no established root system of their own so, unless the proper conditions are provided, they are likely to dehydrate. This is why stem cuttings are often rooted in cups of water or moist soil. Humidity and warm temperatures are also recommended to improve the results of stem cutting propagation.

d.) Step-by-Step Propagation Guides

Step-by Step Guide for Air Layering

Depending on the variety, ficus trees can sometimes be difficult to propagate with cuttings. In cases like this, air layering may be a better option.

1. Choose a stem that is about as wide as a pencil to use for propagation and select an area just below a leaf node

2. Remove all the leaves 4 inches above and 4 inches below this node

3. Score the stem with a sharp knife, making one mark just below the node and a second about a ½ inch

below the first notch

4. Cut away the bark between these two notches and apply a light coating of rooting hormone powder

5. Wrap a sheet of plastic film around the stem about 4 inches below the wound and tie it tightly at the bottom

6. Fill the plastic film with moistened sphagnum moss, packing it in around the wounded stem

7. Tie the top of the plastic film to the stem several inches above the wound to form a sealed ball

8. Wait until new roots begin to poke through the wound and into the sphagnum moss

9. Remove the plastic and sever the stem from the tree just below the root ball

10. Plant the stem in a new pot and resume regular care of your new ficus tree

Step-by-Step Guide for Stem Cutting

There are two ways to root stem cuttings for ficus trees – in water or in soil. In many cases, root growth for cuttings started in water is weak, so soil rooting is preferred.

1. In a small pot, combine equal parts peat moss, vermiculite, and sand to create a well-draining rooting medium

2. Moisten the soil until the extra water drains out the bottom of the pot then let it sit for about an hour

3. Select a stem for your cutting – it should be taken from the tip of a branch with leaves on the end

4. Cut a 4 to 5 inch (10 to 13 cm) length of the stem using a sharp knife to make a clean cut

5. Remove the leaves from the bottom half of the stem and dip the cut end in rooting hormone

6. Place the stem in the pot of rooting medium

7. Drive four sticks into the rooting medium, spacing them evenly around the edges of the pot

8. Lay a piece of clear plastic over the sticks to create a small greenhouse – this will help keep the humidity up for the cutting

9. Place the pot in an area that gets plenty of sunlight, ideally filtered through a window

10. Spray the cutting daily until it starts to show signs of new growth then continue your regular care of your new ficus tree

*Note: Do not seal the plastic around the pot – this could result in the humidity becoming too high which could lead to mold. New cuttings require good airflow to prevent disease.

Chapter Five: Growing Bonsai Ficus

The art of bonsai is simply the reproduction of natural trees, but in miniature form. This practice has been followed for centuries in China and Japan, but it continues to be popular today. If you like the idea of keeping a ficus, but don't have room for a full-grown tree in your house then a bonsai ficus might be a good choice. Keep in mind that bonsai tree care requirements are different from traditional ficus, so read up before you start. In this chapter you will find basic information about starting a bonsai tree, maintaining it, as well as tips for trimming and pruning it.

1.) Selecting a Container

The literal translation for the word "bonsai" is "plantings in tray". If you have ever seen a bonsai tree, you may have noticed that the containers in which they are kept are shallow – very much different from the deep pots used to house traditional ficus trees. Choosing the right container for your bonsai tree is very important – follow these tips to select the best container for your bonsai:

1.) Consider the dimensions of the container in comparison to the dimensions of the tree – the depth should be about equal to the diameter of the trunk at soil level and the width should be about 2/3 the height of the tree

2.) If you are keeping a bonsai ficus with a very wide canopy, you may need a wider pot (you may need to compensate for the extra width by using a slightly shallower pot)

3.) The shape of the pot you choose should be in harmony with the shape of the tree – take a look at the tree to determine whether it has masculine or feminine features and choose your pot accordingly

4.) Masculine features (heavy trunk, craggy bark, angular branches) are best suited to deeper, more angular pots

5.) Feminine features (smooth trunk line, smooth bark, light canopy) are best suited to shallower pots with softer lines

6.) Choose the color of your pot based on what will bring out the features of your tree – select a color that complements the color of the tree's bark

7.) Select a texture for your pot to complement the features of the tree – smooth finishes are ideal for feminine features while coarsely textured finishes are best for masculine features

*Note: The container you choose for your bonsai tree is entirely up to you, but these tips will help you to make a decision. Remember, bonsai is traditionally considered a form of art, so choosing the right pot is an essential part of cultivating your bonsai.

2.) Lighting Requirements

Compared to other bonsai trees, ficus bonsai trees require relatively low levels of light. This makes them one of the easiest varieties of bonsai to keep successfully indoors. Though the exact lighting requirements for bonsai ficus may vary slightly depending on the variety, bonsai trees tend to do best in indirect sunlight. Position your bonsai ficus in a location where it will get plenty of morning light, but will be protected from direct afternoon sun which can burn the leaves.

Follow these tips for ensuring that your bonsai ficus gets enough (but not too much) light:

- Keep the bonsai in a room with south-facing windows, that gets plenty of sun throughout the day

- Place the bonsai on a table or counter within 3 feet of the window – the intensity of sunlight decreases by half for every 3 feet of distance

- Consider placing your bonsai near artificial lighting to ensure that it gets enough light

- Watch your bonsai for signs of inadequate lighting and make adjustments accordingly – in low light conditions, the leaves will become larger and the branches more leggy

- Lighting is most important for bonsai ficus during the spring and summer months when your tree will do most of its growing

- During the winter, a south-facing window that receives at least 4 to 6 hours of sunlight a day is fine

3.) Watering and Feeding

Watering a bonsai ficus is not especially difficult – you just need to keep an eye on the soil and water it before it completely dries out. Many inexperienced bonsai owners kill their first tree by either watering it too much or not watering it enough. Follow these simple tips to ensure that your bonsai is properly watered:

- The best water for a bonsai ficus is soft, room-temperature water

- Feel the soil to a depth of an inch or so – if it feels dry, water the bonsai

- Soak the bonsai in a container of water (up to the level of the trunk) for 5 to 10 minutes, then let it drain

- If you prefer to top water your bonsai, add small amounts at a time and wait a few minutes between each watering to let it soak in

- Keep a spray bottle of water near your ficus bonsai so you have easy access to it

- Lightly mist your bonsai tree once a day to help maintain the proper level of humidity

- Avoid over-misting your bonsai because this could lead to fungal growth

- Keep in mind that the warmer the temperature where your ficus bonsai is kept, the more water it will need

- If you keep your bonsai in a cooler area during the winter, it will only need occasional watering to keep the soil moist

In terms of feeding or fertilizing your bonsai tree, you should plan to do so about every two weeks during the growing season. To fertilize your bonsai, simply dilute a liquid fertilizer with the water you are using to water your bonsai every 2 to 4 weeks during the growing season. See the information in Chapter Four to determine the right fertilizer for your bonsai ficus.

4.) Repotting Bonsai Ficus

As is true for traditional ficus trees, your bonsai ficus will need to be repotted every 1 to 2 years. You will know that it is time to repot your bonsai when the root system has entirely filled the pot. Keep in mind that while a portion of the ficus' root system will be visible above ground, most root growth occurs below ground level. If you do not repot your ficus bonsai often enough, it will become root bound and may fail to thrive.

For the safety of your bonsai, you should plan your repotting for the spring or mid-summer so the tree has time to adjust to the new pot before it goes dormant during the winter. To repot your ficus bonsai, follow these steps:

1.) Carefully remove the bonsai tree along with its soil from the current pot

2.) Rake the soil carefully away from the root ball and prune back the outer and bottom ¼ of the root mass

3.) Place a piece of screen over the drainage holes in the new, slightly larger pot, and cover it with a layer of fine gravel to assist in draining

4.) Add the new soil to the pot to elevate the tree to the right height, then place the tree in the pot

5.) Fill in the area around the tree and the root ball with fresh soil, working it in and under the root mass to avoid leaving any air pockets

6.) Thoroughly water the bonsai by submerging the pot in a tub of water then let it drain

5.) Trimming and Pruning

Pruning a bonsai ficus is very different from pruning a traditional ficus. Whereas for a traditional ficus pruning may be used to only control growth, in a bonsai ficus it is also used to shape and train the tree. In order to keep your ficus in its miniature form, you will need to pinch back or trim new growth, leaving only enough to sustain the health of the tree. Different ficus species will have slightly different growth rates, so you will need to keep an eye on your bonsai throughout the year to determine its pruning and trimming needs.

To properly prune or trim your bonsai ficus, follow the steps below:

1.) Use a pair of small, sharp bonsai scissors to ensure a clean cut

2.) Choose the desired shape for your ficus tree before you begin pruning

3.) Decide which branches you need to remove in order to achieve the desired shape – do not remove more than 50% of the new growth at once

4.) Plan you pruning so that you trim one branch in two that grow opposite each other – this will encourage an alternating branching habit in your bonsai

5.) Start at the bottom of the tree and work your way to the top, following your plan

6.) For major pruning, do it during the winter before new growth in spring

7.) For minor pruning and shaping, prune new growth to maintain the shape of your bonsai

8.) Use pruning shears to remove branches where they connect to the trunk using a downward angled cut

9.) Apply cut paste after removing branches to seal the wound and prevent damage

10.) To remove new growth, pinch off several leaves per shoot, removing them where they connect to the stem

*Note: Regular pruning of your bonsai ficus will not only help to maintain the shape of the tree, but also the size of the leaves. It will take some time for you to get the hang of how to properly prune your bonsai, so err on the side of caution at first and avoid removing too much growth at once until you figure it out.

Chapter Six: Keeping Your Ficus Healthy

Like any living thing, ficus trees have the capacity to get sick. If you are not experienced in caring for houseplants, however, you may not recognized the symptoms and, as a result, your ficus could deteriorate quickly beyond the point of recovery. In this chapter you will learn the basics about how to keep your ficus healthy, including choosing a healthy tree to start with, recognizing the signs of disease, and caring for a sick ficus. The information in this chapter will help you keep your ficus looking great.

1.) Signs of a Healthy Ficus

Unless you are starting your ficus from seed or a cutting, you will most likely be purchasing an established tree. As is true with any living thing that you bring into your household, you should take the time to make sure that your ficus tree is healthy first. If you are inheriting a ficus from a family member or friend, you may not have much say in its current condition but, if you are buying a new tree of your own, follow these tips to bring home a healthy one:

- Buy from a reputable nursery or home and garden store that knows how to care for plants and likely has healthy stock

- View all of the options for ficus trees and decide which variety you are most interested in

- Check the individual ficus trees for general signs of good health and symptoms of illness

- The ficus tree's trunk should be straight and sturdy with no evidence of scars or warping

- The leaves should be rich and green (depending on the variety) with no signs of browning or yellowing

- The soil in the pots should be moist, indicating a well-watered plant, but not wet (if the soil is bone-dry, the plant may be suffering from low water levels)

- You should not see any visible pests in the leaves or soil – if the trees are housed outdoors, you may see a few here and there but a large number may indicate a pest problem

- There should be no signs of recent leaf loss (dead leaves collected in the pot or on the ground) to indicate stress or a recent problem

*Note: If you notice any signs of poor health in a ficus you are considering buying, walk away. Even though you may be able to revive the ficus or remedy the problem, a ficus that has been sick once may be more prone to illness in the future. It may also have been weakened by the disease and may be more sensitive to changes in temperature, humidity, and other environmental factors in the future.

2.) Common Health Problems

For houseplants like the ficus, many health problems are caused directly or indirectly, by insect pests. Insects that feed on the ficus may weaken it, leaving it more susceptible to health problems like mold. The key to keeping your ficus tree healthy is to familiarize yourself with the common pests and health problems you may encounter. The more prepared you are with knowledge about these problems, the better equipped you will be to handle them. In the following pages you will find information about common problems and how to deal with them.

Some of the most common health problems to affect ficus trees include:

- Anthracnose
- Bacterial Leaf Spot
- Blight
- Branch Dieback
- Cold Injury
- Crown Gall
- Foliar Nematode
- Insect Pests

The insect pests which will be covered in this section include the following:

- Mealybugs
- Scale
- Thrips
- Whiteflies

Anthracnose

This is a type of fungal infection which manifests with necrotic spots forming on the surface of affected leaves. While these spots may start out light in color, they eventually turn dark brown and the affected leaves may die and fall off the plant. The white parts of the leaf (the parts lacking chlorophyll) are particularly susceptible to this type of fungus. *Ficus benjamina* is one species of ficus that is most commonly affected by this disease.

This infection is most commonly caused by either *Glomerella cingulate* or *Colletotrichum* spp. The fungus is most likely to grow in wet, humid conditions – it is also common after the misuse of pesticides have caused tissue damage to the tree. Anthracnose is often seen in ficus cuttings that are kept in conditions that are too moist without adequate air flow. The best way to control this disease is to avoid overwatering and to avoid using overhead irrigation for your ficus plants. Application of a fungicide may be necessary to kill the fungus. Fungicides that have been shown effective include mancozeb, iprodione, pyraclostrobin and azoxystrobin.

Bacterial Leaf Spot

In ficus trees, leaf spot disease can be caused by any number of different bacteria. *Ficus benjamina* and *Ficus netida* are commonly affected by the bacteria *Corynespora cassiicola*. Other bacterial agents that may cause leaf spot include *Xanthomonas campestris* and *Myrothecium roridum*. As suggested by the name, this disease typically manifests in the form of dark, discolored spots on the leaves of affected ficus trees.

Leaf spot caused by *Corynespora cassiicola* bacteria typically cause small reddish spots that appear on young and mature leaves – the spots then expand interveinally, causing the leaves to fall off when the infection becomes severe. Leaf spot caused by *Myrothecium roridum* bacteria results in circular brown lesions about the size of a dime which contain dark black spores. This particular version of leaf spot is most severe when the conditions are warm and humid. For all forms of leaf spot, recommended treatments include avoiding the use of overhead irrigation and treatment with fungicides such as azoxystrobin, fludioxonil, and pyraclostrobin.

Blight

Also referred to as Southern Blight, this is a disease that results in the formation of white, feathery mats on the surface of the soil and on various parts of the plant. These formations are caused by the fungus *Sclerotium rolfsii*. Another type of blight, caused by *Rhizoctonia*, results in brown feathery formations. In either case, the formations form small, circular seed-like structures that house and protect the fungal spores as they grow. This is what makes the disease so hard to kill.

Blight tends to occur and spread rapidly in hot, wet conditions. Though this disease occurs most commonly in the South, if the conditions are right, it can thrive in greenhouses and warmer areas further north. Controlling an outbreak of blight is very difficult – in many cases of commercial production, plants showing symptoms of the disease are discarded. For your own personal use, however, a fungicide drench may be useful in treating blight.

Branch Dieback

This disease can be very devastating to ficus plants, resulting in the loss of large amounts of foliage at once. Branch dieback is often the result of the *Phomopsis* pathogen which attacks ficus trees that have already been weakened by some aspect of poor husbandry. This disease is commonly seen in ficus trees kept in poor soil or an unsuitable climate. It may also attack when the ficus doesn't get enough water, has been subjected to extreme pruning, or is suffering from another infection.

Branch dieback in ficus trees typically manifests in a sort of color progression of the affected leaves. They start out by fading or yellowing, then they may turn brown and fall off the tree completely. Small branches are the next portions of the tree to go, followed by larger branches. If the disease is not treated, it may result in the death of the entire tree (this typically takes 2 to 3 years). If the ficus receives treatment, however, it may sprout new growth below the dead branches which can be pruned away.

Cold Injury

Ficus plants require warm, temperate conditions in order to thrive. If you leave your ficus outdoors during the winter, or if the temperature in your house becomes too low, your ficus may suffer from cold injury. This condition manifests in several different ways. For young leaves, they may start to look puckered and turn brown. Larger, mature leaves may develop brown spots. Eventually, the affected leaves may die and fall off the plant.

The best way to avoid this problem is to keep your ficus indoors where the temperature is consistent. Even when keeping your ficus inside, however, you need to be careful. Do not place the ficus too close to heating or cooling vents and make sure that the room where it is housed never goes below 40°F (4°C). If you do choose to keep your ficus outside during the summer, make sure to bring it inside when the temperatures start to drop – well before the danger of the first frost.

Crown Gall

This disease is caused by the bacteria *Agrobacterium tumefaciens*. Crown gall typically manifests in the form of tumor-like growths (called galls) on the surface of stems or roots of infected plants. These galls can grow either externally or internally, causing a swelling of the stem – in fact, this is often the first symptom of crown gall to be exhibited by infected plants. Unfortunately, this swelling is often passed off as being related to a wound. As a result, the infection grows and spreads in the coming weeks until the gall grows so large that it crushes the plant tissue and blocks water flow to the foliage.

There are no known bactericides that have been proven effective against crown gall in ficus trees. The best way to prevent this condition is to ensure proper sterilization of pruning equipment and to choose healthy, disease-free plants. If you must remove galls, do so by cutting the 1stem several inches below the gall tissue.

Foliar Nematode

Nematodes are microscopic organisms, a type of roundworm that can infect the ficus tree from the inside. The most common nematode to affect ficus trees is Aphelenchoides, which is actually fairly large compared to other nematodes (0.5 to 1.2mm). These nematodes have long, hollow, spear-like mouthparts with which they pierce the cells of the plant and draw out the cell components. Aphelenchoides can live inside the plant tissues or remain on the outside of the plant.

Some common symptoms of foliar nematodes in ficus trees include yellow, brown or black areas of the leaves that look wet as well as yellowing or death of leaves that remain attached to the stem. You may also notice distortion of the leaves or stunting of the entire plant. The best way to treat this problem is to remove infected portions of the plant and to avoid making conditions ideal for the nematodes to spread. Nematodes prefer temperatures between 70° and 75° (21° to 24°C), so raising or lowering the temperature for a period of time may help to kill them.

Insect Pests

Insect pests are not only a nuisance for you, but they can also be very dangerous for your ficus. When pests feed on the inner fluid of your ficus' leaves, they are left to dry out and die. As a result, the ficus may be weakened and more susceptible to secondary health problems such as bacterial or fungal infections.

Below you will find an overview of the most common insect pests affecting ficus trees:

Mealybugs – small, slow-moving insects, mealybugs only measure about 0.2 inches (0.5cm) long. These insects are covered in a white, cottony wax and they tend to feed in very large masses. As they feed, these pests leave behind a sticky substance called honeydew which can attract ants and may increase the growth of mold. Minor problems with mealybugs can be addressed with a hard spray of water, stubborn infestations may require an insecticidal soap spray or use of oil to smother the bugs.

Scale – scale insects are brown in color and usually measure less than ¼ inch (0.63cm) in diameter. These insects are hard to spot but they cause a lot of damage by piercing the leaf and sucking out the inner fluids. This leaves the leaf to dry out, turning yellow or curling up and dying. Scale insects also leave behind honeydew. A hard spray of water may help to remove scale insects as well as the use of insecticidal soaps and sprays.

Thrips – these insects are very tiny and difficult to see – they are also very hard to kill. Thrips tend to feed on the more protected areas of ficus trees, causing the formation of galls. Leaves may become dry and shriveled – you may also see areas of sheen marking the place where thrips wounded the leaf. A hard spray of water will help to remove thrips, though pruning infested foliage is also recommended.

Whitefly – like most other insect pests, whiteflies have sucking mouth parts with which they pierce ficus leaves and drain them of their inner fluids. In heavy infestations, the leaves turn yellow, dry out, and fall off the plant. The honeydew left by these pests may also encourage the growth of sooty mold. The first step in dealing with whiteflies is to wash the plant – insecticidal soaps and products containing neem oil are the second step. In very heavy infestations, you may be able to use a vacuum to suck the insects off the plant – just be sure to seal and freeze the vacuum bag for 24 hours to kill the pests.

3.) Natural Remedies for Pests and Disease

If you want to keep your ficus or bonsai tree healthy, the last thing you want to do is to go spraying it with chemicals. Commercial fungicides, pesticides, and herbicides may be toxic to diseases and pests – but they may be toxic to your ficus as well! In this section you will receive tips and recipes for making your own all-natural remedies for pests and diseases at home. Many of these recipes are made using ingredients you already have – others may simply require a quick trip to the health food store.

a.) Baking Soda Fungicide

This all-natural fungicide is incredibly easy to prepare because you likely already have the ingredients at home. The sooner you catch the signs of fungus, black spot, or mildew and apply this mixture, the more quickly your ficus will recover.

Ingredients:

- 1 tablespoon baking soda
- 1 tablespoon citrus or horticultural oil
- 1 gallon (4.5 litres) water

Instructions:

1.) Combine all of the ingredients in a large spray bottle and shake well.
2.) Spray the mixture over the affected leaves, paying close attention to the underside.
3.) Avoid over-spraying and try not to get any of the mixture into the soil.

b.) Anti-Fungal Compost Tea

If you are worried about using baking soda on your ficus, this compost tea will be just as effective. This mixture works best with compost made from about 75% plant matter (grass clippings, tree trimmers, and vegetable refuse) and 25% animal waste (manure).

Ingredients:

- 5 gallons (23 litres) compost
- 5 gallons (23 litres) water

Instructions:

1.) Fill a 10-gallon (46 litre) bucket about half full with compost and fill it the rest of the way with water.
2.) Let the mixture sit for about two weeks then siphon off the liquid.
3.) Dilute the liquid with fresh water until it is the color of iced tea and pour it into a spray bottle.
4.) Spray the mixture over the affected leaves, paying close attention to the undersides.

c.) Soap Spray for Mealybugs

Mealybugs are tiny insects with long bodies covered in a waxy coating. These insects gather in large masses and can cause severe damage to ficus trees, leading to stunted growth and premature leaf drop. This soap spray is an easy way to discourage these insects from infesting your ficus.

Ingredients:

- 1 quart (1 litre) liquid castile soap
- ½ cup rubbing alcohol

Instructions:

1.) Combine the ingredients in a large spray bottle.
2.) Spray the mixture liberally over the leaves, paying close attention to the underside.
3.) Leave the mixture on for 20 minutes – the alcohol will strip the protective waxy coating from the mealybugs so the soap can penetrate their skin and kill them.
4.) Rinse the ficus well with water to remove the alcohol.
5.) Repeat every three days as long as needed.

d.) Garlic Spray for Scale

Scale insects are tiny and very difficult to spot, but you will have no trouble seeing the damage they leave behind. After these insects suck the fluids from ficus leaves, they leave behind a sticky substance that attracts other insects and allows for sooty mold to grow. This garlic spray helps to deter scale insects and other leaf-eating pests.

Ingredients:

- 4 cups water
- 1 teaspoon dish soap
- 1 bulb garlic, peeled and chopped
- 2 large onions, chopped
- 2 small red or green chillies, chopped

Instructions:

1.) Combine the garlic, onion and chillies in a large bowl.
2.) Mix together the soap and water then pour over the ingredients in the bowl.
3.) Let the mixture steep for 24 hours then strain it into a spray bottle.

4.) Spray the mixture over your ficus, paying special attention to the underside of the leaves.

e.) Oil and Soap Spray for Whiteflies

Whiteflies can be very difficult to control because they reproduce quickly and can even spread to other plants in your house. These insects pierce the leaves of ficus plants and suck out the inner fluids, leaving the foliage to dry out and die. This oil and soap spray is a quick and easy way to deter whiteflies from your ficus.

Ingredients:

- 1 tablespoon mild dish soap
- 1 cup vegetable oil
- Water

Instructions:

1.) Combine the dish soap and vegetable oil in a mixing bowl and whisk until well combined.
2.) Spoon about 1 ½ to 2 teaspoons of the mixture into a spray bottle.
3.) Add 1 cup of water and shake well.

4.) Spray the mixture over your ficus, paying special attention to the underside of the leaves.

5.) For the best results, spray in the early morning and reapply after watering.

Chapter Seven: Relevant Websites

Though this book is full of valuable information about ficus trees and ficus bonsai trees, there may be certain areas in which you are curious for more information. In this chapter you will find lists of relevant websites for further reading in both the U.S. and the U.K. in the following categories:

Ficus Species and Varieties

Ficus Seeds and Plants

Potting and Pruning Supplies

Bonsai Ficus Resources

1.) Ficus Species and Varieties

United States Websites:

"Ficus." The Plant List.

www.theplantlist.org

"Ficus Classification." USDA.

https://plants.usda.gov

"Introduction to Ornamental Figs in Cultivation." Dave's Garden.

http://davesgarden.com

United Kingdom Websites:

Walls-Thumma, Dawn. "How to Identify Ficus Varieties."

www.ehow.co.uk

"Ficus Benjamina." Royal Horticultural Society.

www.rhs.org.uk

"Ficus Bonsai Species Guide." Bonsai4Me.
www.bonsai4me.co.uk

"Figs: Ornamental (Ficus)." Royal Horticultural Society.
https://www.rhs.org.uk

2.) Ficus Seeds and Plants

United States Websites:

"Ficus Retusa Seeds." RareExoticSeeds.
www.rarexoticseeds.com

"Various Ficus Seeds." RarePalmSeeds.
http://bit.ly/rarepalmseeds

"Benjamina Ficus Tree." Fast-Growing-Trees.
www.fast-growing-trees.com

United Kingdom Websites:

"Various Ficus Seeds." BuyitGrowit.
www.buyitgrowit.co.uk

"Ficus microcarpa." House of Plants.
www.houseofplants.co.uk

"Large Assortment of Ficus Plants." Gardens4You.co.uk.
www.gardens4you.co.uk

3.) Potting and Pruning Supplies

United States Websites:

"Pruning Tools and Equipment." Gempler's.
www.gemplers.com

"Pruning Supplies." OBC Northwest, Inc.

http://obcnw.com

United Kingdom Websites:

"Bonsai Tools and Compost" BuyitGrowit.

www.buyitgrowitco.uk

"How to Repot Your Ficus Bonsai." The Garden Prince.

http://thegardenprince.co.uk

4.) Bonsai Ficus Resources

United States Websites:

"Growing Your Ficus Bonsai." Sleepy Hollow Bonsai.
www.shbonsai.com

"Ficus Bonsai Care." Bonsai Outlet.
www.bonsaioutlet.com

"Bonsai Ficus Ginseng." Bonsai Made Easy.
www.bonsai-made-easy.com

United Kingdom Websites:

"Growing and Caring for Bonsai Ficus Trees." Bonsai
Empire.
www.bonsaiempire.com

"Indoor Bonsai Ficus Retusa (Fig Bonsai Tree)." Bonsai
Direct.
http://www.bonsaidirect.co.uk

"Ficus Bonsai Trees." All Things Bonsai.

www.allthingsbonsai.co.uk

"Tree seeds suitable for bonsai" BuyitGrowit.

www.buyitgrowit.co.uk

Photo Credits

Cover Page Photo By Forest & Kim Starr
via Wikimedia Commons. Ficus benjamina.

Page 1 Photo By Tato Grasso
via Wikimedia Commons. Ficus macrophylla.

Page 5 Photo By Vinayaraj
via Wikimedia Commons. Ficus microcarpa.

Page 7 Photo By JMK
via Wikimedia Commons

Page 9 Photo By Slav4
via Wikimedia Commons

Page 13 Photo By Flickr user Koshyk

Page 14 Photo By Forest and Kim Starr
via Wikimedia Commons. Ficus carica.

Page 16 Photo By Forest & Kim Starr
via Wikimedia Commons. Ficus benjamina.

Page 18 Photo By Channer
via Wikimedia Commons. Ficus retusa.

Page 20 Photo By Netrider1964
via Wikimedia Commons. Ficus microcarpa.

Page 22 Photo By Bhaskaranaidu
via Wikimedia Commons. Ficus religiosa.

Page 24 Photo By PikiWiki
via Wikimedia Commons. Ficus microcarpa.

Page 25 Photo By Dedda71
via Wikimedia Commons.

Page 28 Photo By Mo707
via Wikimedia Commons.

Page 33 Photo By Forest & Kim Starr
via Wikimedia Commons. Ficus microcarpa.

Page 38 Photo By Flickr user Madaise
via Wikimedia Commons.

Page 40 Photo By Andreaskrappweis
via Wikimedia Commons. Ficus religiosa.

Page 49 Photo By Rob Hille
via Wikimedia Commons. Ficus indica.

Page 54 Photo By Glmory
via Wikimedia Commons. Ficus benghalensis.

Page 63 Photo By RTG
via Wikimedia Commons. Ficus religiosa

Page 68 Photo By Missvain
via Wikimedia Commons. Ficus microcarpa.

Page 71 Photo By Piotrus
via Wikimedia Commons. Ficus benjamina.

Page 75 Photo "Bonsai Tree 071". Licensed under Creative
Commons Attribution-Share Alike 2.5 via Wikimedia
Commons.

Page 77 Photo By Piotrus
via Wikimedia Commons. Ficus microcarpa.

Page 80 Photo By Eric Guinther
via Wikimedia Commons. Ficus religiosa.

Page 83 Photo By Dr. S. Soundarapandian
via Wikimedia Commons

Page 94 Photo via BigStockPhoto.net

Page 101 Photo By Etienne
via Wikimedia Commons

Resources

Arbuckle, Kit. "How to Prune Branches on a Bonsai Ficus." SFGate Home Guides.

http://homeguides.sfgate.com

"Care Guide for the Ficus Bonsai Tree." Bonsai Empire.

www.bonsaiempire.com

"Choosing the Right Pot for Your Bonsai." Bonsai4Me.com.

www.bonsai4me.com

"Ficus Ginseng Gardening – Basic Tips." Ficus Ginseng.

www.ficusginseng.org

"Ficus Microcarpa." Plants Rescue.

http://plantsrescue.com

"Ficus Plant Care and Feeding." Martha Stewart.

www.marthastewart.com

"Ficus Production Guide." University of Florida IFAS.

http://mrec.ifas.ufl.edu/Foliage/folnotes/ficus.htm

"Ficus Religiosa." Missouri Botanical Garden.

www.missouribotanicalgarden.org

"Figs." Plant Care Guides,
www.garden.org

"How to Prune a Ficus Benjamina Tree." TreeRemoval.com.
www.treeremoval.com

"Ornamental Ficus Diseases: Identification and Control in
Commercial Greenhouse Operations." University of Florida
IFAS Extension. http://edis.ifas.ufl.edu/pp308

"USDA Plant Hardiness Zone Map." USDA.gov.
http://planthardiness.ars.usda.gov/PHZMWeb/

"Weeping Fig Plant." House Plants Expert.
http://www.houseplantsexpert.com

Index

E

epiphyte — 3
evergreen — 6, 18, 22, 46

F

fertilizer — 32, 42, 45, 52, 53, 54, 55, 72
fig — 1, 3, 7, 8, 10, 11, 12, 15, 39, 48, 101, 106, 111, 115
flowers — 3, 4, 7, 8, 10, 100
foliage — 2, 3, 54, 86, 88, 91, 97, 108
Foliar Nematode — 82, 89
fruit — 1, 5, 8, 9, 10, 12, 14, 15, 16, 44
fungicide — 83, 85, 93
fungus — 83, 85, 93

G

germinate — 3, 101, 114
Ginseng Fig — 5
growing season — 34, 37, 42, 52, 55, 60, 72

H

hardiness zone — 26
healthy — 30, 49, 54, 78, 79, 81, 88, 92
height — 14, 16, 20, 29, 67, 74
history — 3, 9, 11, 121
humidity — 25, 37, 41, 45, 46, 65, 72, 80

I

indoors — 2, 17, 23, 25, 27, 28, 29, 33, 34, 36, 38, 43, 44, 46, 48, 50, 69, 87, 113, 121
inflorescence — 3, 4, 7, 8, 10
Insect Pests — 82, 90

L

M

N

O

P

Q

R

S

T

W

Notes:

CPSIA information can be obtained
at www.ICGtesting.com
Printed in the USA
BVHW061142170119
538032BV00012B/220/P